MW01092969

Project-Based Activities
Grades 6–8
English Language Arts Series

Authors: Schyrlet Cameron and Carolyn Craig
Editor: Mary Dieterich
Proofreaders: Cindy Neisen and Margaret Brown

COPYRIGHT © 2017 Mark Twain Media, Inc.

ISBN 978-1-62223-633-6

Printing No. CD-404254

Mark Twain Media, Inc., Publishers
Distributed by Carson-Dellosa Publishing LLC

Table of Contents

To the Teacher

Motivating students is one of the basic challenges facing middle-school teachers. Research indicates students are motivated to learn if the topic is interesting and relevant. *Project-Based Activities, Grades 6–8* is a dynamic approach to learning in which students explore meaningful real-world problems relevant to their lives. The project activities engage students in learning that goes beyond recall and copying information. They give students a reason for learning important concepts and skills.

The English Language Arts Common Core State Standards stress the importance of students being able to "read analytically, write effectively, speak and listen purposefully, and conduct research" and to "use technology and digital media strategically and capably." This book is designed to allow students to develop and practice these essential skills while creating high-quality, authentic products and presentations. Project activities vary in length, from several days to several weeks or even a semester. Activities involve students working independently, in collaborative teams, or as a whole class, researching an essential question, creating a multimedia product, and presenting the project to an audience.

The book contains six student-centered, interdisciplinary units. The content of each unit is correlated to the English Language Arts Common Core State Standards. For each unit, the book includes the following sections:

- **Teacher Information:** identifies the project overview, objectives, integration of other academic skills, materials and resources needed, technology requirements, steps for managing the project, and Common Core State Standards correlation

- **Student Project Planner:** presents project overview and directions for the students

- **Mini Lessons:** reviews concepts and skills needed as a result of the project assignment

- **Project Rubric:** explains the set of criteria used for assessing the project

- **Student Self-evaluation and Reflection:** asks students to think about what and how they are learning

What Are Project-Based Activities?

Project-based activities are authentic, engaging, and stimulating learning tasks. The activities are content-based and designed to reflect the types of work people do in the everyday world outside the classroom. The high-interest topics lead students to develop valuable workplace skills including communication and collaboration, organization and time management, questioning and problem-solving, investigation and research, and self-assessment and reflection.

Using Project-Based Activities

Projects address relevant issues and focus on research and writing skills. They require students to use technology and digital media to create and present their projects to audiences beyond the classroom.

The projects can be effective at all grade levels and with all subject areas and instructional programs, including after-school and alternative programs. The projects are generally done by teams of students working together to solve a problem and formulate a solution. Projects vary in length from several days to several weeks or even a semester.

How to Assess Learning

A teacher evaluation along with student reflection and self-evaluation are important components of each project. Student performance is assessed on an individual basis and takes into account the quality of the product produced, the depth of content understanding demonstrated, and the contributions made to the project.

Implementing Project-Based Activities

Step 1—Introduction: The teacher launches the project with an event such as a video, discussion, guest speaker, field trip, or scenario.

Step 2—Essential Question: The teacher presents a question that will be the focus of the project.

Step 3—Research and Write: Students research the essential question, discover answers, draw conclusions, and generate solutions.

Step 4—Product: Students create a product such as a book trailer or virtual museum, using the Internet and technology.

Step 5—Presentation: Students share their project with the appropriate audience, such as middle-school staff, parents, or the community.

Step 6—Evaluation and Reflection: The teacher and student both assess learning and performance using a rubric, teacher feedback, and student self-evaluation and reflection.

Unit 1: Anti-Bullying Campaign—Teacher Information

Project Overview
Students will use the Internet to research and produce an anti-bullying graphic novel.

Project Objectives
When students complete this project, they will be able to • write a story. • create a graphic novel. • use technology to create and share the graphic novel.

Integration of Academic Skills
• Language Arts: write a narrative • Technology: use computer word processing, graphic programs, online resources

Primary Common Core State Standards Addressed		
ELA-Literacy.W.6.3 Write narratives to develop real or imagined experiences or events using effective technique, relevant descriptive details, and well-structured event sequences. ELA-Literacy.W.6.6 Use technology, including the Internet, to produce and publish writing as well as to interact and collaborate with others; demonstrate sufficient command of keyboarding skills to type a minimum of three pages in a single sitting.	ELA-Literacy.W.7.3 Write narratives to develop real or imagined experiences or events using effective technique, relevant descriptive details, and well-structured event sequences. ELA-Literacy.W.7.6 Use technology, including the Internet, to produce and publish writing and link to and cite sources as well as to interact and collaborate with others, including linking to and citing sources.	ELA-Literacy.W.8.3 Write narratives to develop real or imagined experiences or events using effective technique, relevant descriptive details, and well-structured event sequences. ELA-Literacy.W.8.6 Use technology, including the Internet, to produce and publish writing and present the relationships between information and ideas efficiently as well as to interact and collaborate with others.

Essential Question	Type of Project
What can be done to prevent bullying at our school?	■ Individual Student ☐ Collaborative Teams ☐ Whole Class

Introductory Event
1. *Scenario:* The National Education Association reports that bullying is the number one discipline problem in middle schools. Parents and faculty want to mobilize students to work on an anti-bullying initiative. 2. *Discussion:* Ask students how they would define bullying, and write definitions or words on the board addressing the different kinds of bullying (teasing, name-calling, rumors, etc.). 3. *Activity:* Students go online to the URL <http://www.tolerance.org/lesson/bullying-quiz> and complete the quiz. Then involve students in a follow-up discussion about bullying. 4. *Activity:* Display a variety of graphic novels. Give students time to examine the novels. Discuss how the visuals support each aspect of the narrative.

Unit 1: Anti-Bullying Campaign—Teacher Information

Materials/Resources Needed
1. A copy of all handouts for each student: There are several options—paper copy, scan and download handouts to be used on a whiteboard, or post handouts to the classroom web page to be downloaded by students to their laptops.   2. A variety of graphic novels for students to preview

Technology
1. Computers with word processing, printer, and graphic programs   2. Computers with Internet connections

Internet Tools for Creating Comic Strips for a Graphic Novel
The following sites offer tools for creating comic strips that can be printed and organized into a graphic novel.   URL: <http://www.makebeliefscomix.com>   Make Beliefs Comix is free and doesn't require a user account to create a comic. Publishing is done by printing or saving as a PDF.   URL: <http://www.toondoo.com/createToon.do>   Toondoo offers a free creator with options for customizing characters, adding images, and multiple frame selections. Publishing is done by printing or saving as a PDF.

Managing the Project
Step 1: Launch Project–Discuss the essential question, and complete the introductory activities.   Step 2: Review–"Graphic Novel Project Rubric" and "Project Self-Evaluation and Reflection" handouts   Step 3: Review–"Project Planner" handout   Step 4: Activity–Students research bullying.   Step 5: Mini-Lesson–"Parts of a Graphic Novel" handout   Step 6: Mini-Lesson–"Parts of a Story" handout   Step 7: Mini-Lesson–"Story Setting" handout   Step 8: Activity–"Creating Unforgettable Characters" and "Protagonist vs. Antagonist" handouts   Step 9: Activity–Students write their stories.   Step 10: Activity–"Graphic Novel Storyboard" handout.   Step 11: Activity–Students create their graphic novels. Some students may wish to create a hand-illustrated novel, while others may want to create the novel using Microsoft Word or one of the comic generators listed in the "Materials/Resources" section above. If an online comic generator is used, students should be sure to print out the comics as necessary. Various pages can be assembled into a graphic novel using some old-fashioned cutting-and-pasting (or digital work). All novels need to be scanned or saved to a computer to be uploaded to the classroom web page so other students can access and read.   Step 12: Activity–Collaborate with the school librarian to host a "Graphic Novel Exhibition."

Project Evaluation
1. The teacher completes the "Graphic Novel Project Rubric" handout for each student.   2. Students complete the "Project Self-Evaluation and Reflection" handout.   3. Teacher/student conferences are held to discuss the completed evaluations.

Name: _____

Date: _____

Graphic Novel Project Rubric

Components	Advanced	Proficient	Nearing Proficient	Below Proficient	
Narrative	Story has a clear introduction, plot development, and conclusion. Dialogue is relevant to pictures.	Story has an introduction, plot, and conclusion. Dialogue not always relevant to pictures.	Story has an introduction, but no real development of plot or conclusion. Missing key elements. Dialogue has little to do with pictures.	Story does not appear to have any clear introduction, plot, or conclusion. Dialogue doesn't match pictures.	
Language and Mechanics	Demonstrates command of writing conventions: spelling, capitalization, punctuation, and/or grammar.	Little need for editing in spelling, capitalization, punctuation, and/or grammar.	Contains careless or distracting errors in spelling, capitalization, punctuation, and/or grammar.	Contains many errors in spelling, capitalization, punctuation, and/or grammar.	
Cover	Clearly communicates what the book is about while grabbing the reader's attention.	Communicates what the book is about.	Difficult to determine what the book is about from the cover.	Cover has no relationship to the story.	
Title Page	Title page has eye-catching graphics, a title, author and illustrator's name, and year.	Title page has graphics, title, author and illustrator's name, and year.	Has title page but missing one or more of the required elements.	Does not have a title page.	
Images	Graphics enhance the story and are appropriate for the dialogue.	Graphics are appropriate for the story and dialogue.	Graphics are inappropriate and do little to enhance the story.	Graphics detract from the story.	
Layout	Logical flow of pictures and dialogue; effective use of page panels, speech and thought balloons.	Pictures in sequence with dialogue, adequate use of page panels, speech and thought balloons.	Layout of pictures and text confusing. Page panels do not support flow of story. Has speech and thought balloons.	Layout distracting or does not tell a clear story.	
Presentation	The graphic novel is easy to read and all elements are clearly written, labeled, or drawn.	The graphic novel is easy to read and most elements are clearly written, labeled, or drawn.	The graphic novel is hard to read with small fonts and may have poor color choices.	The graphic novel is hard to read. There seems to be no logical design.	

Teacher Comments:

Name: _____ Date: _____

Project Self-Evaluation and Reflection

Project Title: _____

Write a brief summary of the project.

List three things you learned while working on the project. Place a star by the most important thing you learned.

1. _____

_____

2. _____

_____

3. _____

_____

What do you wish you had done differently?

How would you evaluate your work? (Check One)

_____ Unsatisfactory

_____ Poor

_____ Average

_____ Good

_____ Excellent

Unit 1: Anti-Bullying Campaign—Student Project Planner

Essential Question: What can be done to prevent bullying at our school?

Project: Research bullying. Use the information and your personal experiences to create a graphic novel that presents the consequences of bullying and offers possible solutions for the problem.

Steps

Step 1: Review the "Graphic Novel Project Rubric" and "Project Self-Evaluation and Reflection" handouts.

Step 2: Go online to the URL addresses below. Research bullying to gain a better understanding of the problem and learn about possible solutions.

URL: <http://www.stopbullying.gov/kids/index.html>
URL: <https://nces.ed.gov/fastfacts/display.asp?id=719>
URL: <http://www.stopbullying.gov/news/media/facts/>

Step 3: Review the "Parts of a Graphic Novel," "Parts of a Story," "Story Setting," and "Creating Unforgettable Characters" handouts.

Step 4: Complete the "Plotting a Story" and "Protagonist vs. Antagonist" handouts.

Step 5: Write your story. Use the handouts listed above to help you.

Step 6: Use the story you wrote to complete the "Graphic Novel Storyboard" handout.

Step 7: Create your graphic novel. Design the cover and title page. Craft the pages for your novel using your completed "Graphic Novel Storyboard" handout. There are several options for the project, from hand-illustrating your novel to using an online comic generator. Consult with your teacher for guidelines.

Step 8: Share your completed project by uploading it to the classroom web page.

Step 9: Work with your classmates and the school librarian to create a graphic novel exhibition.

Step 10: Complete the "Project Self-Evaluation and Reflection" handout.

Unit 1: Anti-Bullying Campaign—Parts of a Graphic Novel

A **graphic novel** is a story that is created using a comic-strip format and published as a book.

Cover: The cover includes the front and back sides of the book. The design should clearly communicate what the book is about while grabbing the reader's attention.

Title Page: The title page lists the name of the book, author, illustrator, and the copyright date (the date the book was written or published).

Panels: The most common page layout is the 6-panel grid. The individual panels, when put together, tell the story in sequential order.

Examples: The panels may be combined in a variety of ways.

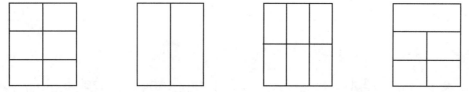

Splash Page: This page is one panel that takes up the entire page. It is used to help introduce the story or give special attention to an event.

Borders and Gutters:

Gutters: space between the panels (shaded gray in this example).

Border: outline of the page

Text: The words that make up the graphic novel are called the text. It is organized in a specific way.

Balloons: The bubbles that contain the dialogue and thoughts of the characters.

Caption: The text that is directed to the reader. It often appears below the comic panel.

Narrator Blocks: The rectangles or squares above the comic panel. Gives an explanation of what is happening in the panel.

Sound Effects: The words or letters that stand for sounds.

Max couldn't wait to use his new hand lens.

What big teeth you have!

GR-R-R-R!

Where's my treat?

Bared fangs are a sure sign of an angry dog.

Unit 1: Anti-Bullying Campaign—Parts of a Story

A **story** is a narrative made up by the author. Every story has the same three basic parts: setting, characters, and plot. These three elements work together to grab and hold the reader's interest.

SETTING: where and when the story takes place. The setting includes location, weather, time of day, and time period.

CHARACTERS: a person, animal, or imaginary creature in your story. There are usually one or two main characters. Writers develop story characters in four ways: appearance, actions, and what they say and think.

PLOT: the sequence of events in a story. The plot has a beginning, a middle, and an end.

Beginning	Middle	End
The beginning of the story introduces the characters, describes the setting, establishes the problem, and gets the readers interested in the story. A good beginning: • grabs the reader's attention right away • might start with a question • might make a statement that surprises the reader • might start with a character's words (dialogue)	The following things happen in the middle of a story. • The problem gets worse. • Roadblocks continually get in the way for the main character. • More information is revealed about the characters. • The middle is the longest part. • The reader really becomes "hooked" on the story and empathizes with the characters and their problems.	The following things happen in the ending of a story. • The problem is resolved. • The loose ends are tied up. • Readers feel that the story is finished; they feel satisfied with the ending.

Name: _____   Date: _____

Unit 1: Anti-Bullying Campaign—Story Setting

> The **setting** gives your story a place and time to happen. It has a huge effect on the mood (atmosphere) of the narrative. Writers reveal the setting through details within the story.

Good writers pay close attention to the unique details of the setting. They use vivid language to describe the location and time of the story.

Location settings to consider:
- a country, state, region, city, or town
- neighborhood, school, or a street
- urban city, a farm, forest, or mountains

Time settings to consider:
- Time of day: morning, the middle of the day, at night
- Time of year: summer, winter, spring, fall
- Holiday: 4th of July, Halloween, Christmas
- Historical event: American Revolution, Civil War, Great Depression

Details within the story:
- use vivid language
- choose nouns and descriptive adjectives
- use action verbs
- use sensory details including sight, sound, touch, smell, and taste

Directions: Read the excerpt from the novel *White Fang,* and then answer the questions and follow the directions below.

> **Text:** *White Fang* by Jack London (excerpt)
>
> Dark spruce forest frowned on either side the frozen waterway. The trees had been stripped by a recent wind of their white covering of frost, and they seemed to lean towards each other, black and ominous, in the fading light. A vast silence reigned over the land. The land itself was desolation, lifeless, without movement, so lone and cold that the spirit of it was not even that of sadness. It was the WILD, the savage, frozen-hearted Northland Wild.
>
> *Public Domain*

1. Where is the location of the place being described in the excerpt?

   _____

2. When is the scene taking place? _____

3. Circle a descriptive adjective used by the author to describe the setting.

4. Underline an example of a sensory detail used by the author to describe the setting.

Unit 1: Anti-Bullying Campaign— Creating Unforgettable Characters

A **character** is a person (human, animal, or creature) that interacts with others within a story. One way the reader learns about a character is by the choice of words the writer uses to describe the appearance and personality of the person.

Character traits are elements of a character's personality. To show what a character is like, a writer uses descriptive words such as *arrogant, easy-going,* and *reliable.*

adventurous	fearless	jovial	responsible
aggressive	fierce	kind	rude
angry	generous	lazy	selfish
argumentative	gloomy	light-hearted	serious
bold	greedy	lovable	silly
bossy	grouchy	malicious	smart
brave	happy	mean	thoughtful
cheerful	hateful	mischievous	timid
courageous	honest	nervous	understanding
cowardly	immature	obnoxious	unfriendly
dependable	impatient	optimistic	vain
dishonest	impulsive	patient	wise
encouraging	intelligent	polite	witty
energetic	inventive	proud	yielding
faithful	jealous	respectful	zany

Physical characteristics refer to the appearance of a character. To show what a character looks like, a writer uses descriptive words such as *tall, scrawny,* or *unkempt.*

Physical Characteristic	Descriptive Words
Eye	*large, blue-green, hazel, glasses, squinty, round, bright, dull, beady*
Height	*tall, short, average, petite, tiny*
Weight	*fat, skinny, athletic, muscular*
Hair	*short, ponytail, redhead, messy, neat, greasy, straight, straggly*
Eyebrows	*arched, full, thick, thin, dark, bushy, unruly*
Skin	*flabby, leathery, dimpled, freckled, tattooed, scarred, pale, olive, peach*
Nose	*turned-up, flat, straight, hooked, crooked snub, dainty, button*
Mouth	*thin, down-turned, cracked, large, wide, red, gaping*
Lips	*narrow, full, pale, chapped, rough, smooth*
Teeth	*missing, bucked, yellow, white, gapped*

11

Name: _____   Date: _____

Unit 1: Anti-Bullying Campaign—Protagonist vs. Antagonist

> The main character in a story is generally known as the **protagonist**; the character who opposes this person is the **antagonist**.

Directions: Complete the graphic organizer for the protagonist and antagonist in your story.

Protagonist	Antagonist
Name: _____	Name: _____
Gender: (circle one) boy girl man woman	Gender: (circle one) boy girl man woman
Age: (circle one) child teen adult	Age: (circle one) child teen adult
Character Traits	**Character Traits**
Physical Characteristics	**Physical Characteristics**
Sketch	**Sketch**

Name: _____ Date: _____

Unit 1: Anti-Bullying Campaign—Graphic Novel Storyboard

A **storyboard** is a graphic organizer. It is an easy way to plan the pictures and text needed for each panel of your graphic novel.

Directions: Use the story you wrote to complete the storyboard. You will need more than one copy of this page.

Describe Graphics Needed:	Describe Graphics Needed:	Describe Graphics Needed:
Narrator Block (if needed):	Narrator Block (if needed):	Narrator Block (if needed):
Action:	Action:	Action:
Dialogue:	Dialogue:	Dialogue:
Sound Effects (if needed):	Sound Effects (if needed):	Sound Effects (if needed):
Caption (if needed):	Caption (if needed):	Caption (if needed):

13

Unit 2: School Brochures—Teacher Information

Project Overview

Students will research their school. They will use the information to create an informational brochure promoting the school.

Project Objectives

When students complete this project, they will be able to
- write an informational brochure.
- use technology to produce and publish a brochure.

Integration of Academic Skills

- Language Arts: write informational text
- Technology: use computer word processing, graphic programs, online resources

Primary Common Core State Standards Addressed

ELA-Literacy.W.6.2 Write informative/explanatory texts to examine a topic and convey ideas, concepts, and information through the selection, organization, and analysis of relevant content. ELA-Literacy.W.6.6 Use technology, including the Internet, to produce and publish writing as well as to interact and collaborate with others; demonstrate sufficient command of keyboarding skills to type a minimum of three pages in a single sitting.	ELA-Literacy.W.7.2 Write informative/explanatory texts to examine a topic and convey ideas, concepts, and information through the selection, organization, and analysis of relevant content. ELA-Literacy.W.7.6 Use technology, including the Internet, to produce and publish writing and link to and cite sources as well as to interact and collaborate with others, including linking to and citing sources.	CCSS.ELA-Literacy.W.8.2 Write informative/explanatory texts to examine a topic and convey ideas, concepts, and information through the selection, organization, and analysis of relevant content. ELA-Literacy.W.8.6 Use technology, including the Internet, to produce and publish writing and present the relationships between information and ideas efficiently as well as to interact and collaborate with others.

© Copyright 2010. National Governors Association Center for Best Practices and Council of Chief State School Officers. All rights reserved.

Essential Question	Type of Project
What can be done to promote our school?	■ Individual Student ☐ Collaborative Teams ☐ Whole Class

Introductory Event

1. *Scenario:* Middle-school students want to promote their school.
2. *Discussion:* As a class, discuss what students know about their school.
3. *Activity:* Generate a list of school information such as after-school programs, extracurricular activities, and notable school history.
4. *Activity:* Invite a local realtor to share knowledge about what people look for when moving to a new community.
5. *Activity:* Display a variety of brochures. Give students time to examine the brochures. Discuss how the print and graphic features support the purpose of the brochure.

Unit 2: School Brochures—Teacher Information

Materials/Resources Needed
1. A copy of all handouts for each student: There are several options—paper copy, scan and download handouts to be used on a whiteboard, or post handouts to the classroom web page to be downloaded by students to their laptops.   2. A variety of brochures for students to preview

Technology
1. Computers with word processing, printer, and graphic programs   2. Computers with Internet connections

Internet Tools for Creating a Brochure
The following sites offer tools for creating brochures.
URL: <https://www.canva.com/create/brochures/>   Canva is a free site that allows students to customize a brochure in four simple steps. Brochures can also be saved and shared. No need to download or install anything.
Google Docs offers a variety of free brochure templates. To access the templates you will need a Google account. A Google account is a unified sign-in system that gives one access to Google products like Docs.

Managing the Project
Step 1: Launch Project—Discuss the essential question, and complete the introductory activities.   Step 2: Review—"School Brochures Project Rubric" handout and "Project Self-Evaluation and Reflections" handout (located on page 6)   Step 3: Review—"Student Project Planner" handout   Step 4: Mini-Lesson—"What is Informational Text?" handout   Step 5: Activity—"Investigating Brochures" handout   Step 6: Mini-Lessons—"Tri-fold Brochure" and "Creating an Effective Informational Brochure" handouts   Step 7: Activity—Students conduct their school research using "School Research" handout.   Step 8: Activity—Students create a rough draft of their brochure using the "Brochure Template" handout.   Step 9: Activity—Students use their completed "School Research" handout and an online brochure maker or a computer program such as Microsoft Word to create their brochure.   Step 10: Activity—Students print brochures to share with a local real estate office and the central school office. Brochures may also be shared on the classroom or school web page and/or linked to local real estate offices.

Project Evaluation
1. The teacher completes the "School Brochures Project Rubric" handout for each student.   2. Students complete the "Project Self-Evaluation and Reflection" handout (page 6).   3. Teacher/student conferences are held to discuss the completed evaluations.

Name: _____   Date: _____

School Brochures Project Rubric

Components	Advanced 1	Proficient 2	Nearing Proficient 3	Below Proficient 4
Purpose	Fully understands the purpose for writing an informational brochure.	Mostly understands the purpose for writing an informational brochure.	Somewhat understands the purpose for writing an informational brochure.	Little understanding of the purpose for writing an informational brochure.
Layout and Design	All steps followed in the "Brochure Template" handout.	Most steps followed in the "Brochure Template" handout.	Some steps followed in the "Brochure Template" handout.	Few steps followed in the "Brochure Template" handout.
Print and Graphic Text Features	Brochure is eye-catching and uses print and graphic text features to enhance all information.	Brochure is mostly eye-catching and uses print and graphic text features to enhance most information.	Brochure is somewhat eye-catching and uses print and graphic text features to enhance some information.	Brochure is not eye-catching, and print and graphic text features do not enhance information.
Language and Mechanics	Writer demonstrates command of conventions; correct grammar and rules for capitalization, punctuation, and spelling.	Brochure is written with little need for editing in spelling, capitalization, punctuation, and/or grammar.	Brochure contains careless or distracting errors in spelling, capitalization, punctuation, and/or grammar.	Brochure contains many errors in spelling, capitalization, punctuation, and/or grammar.

Teacher Comments:

Unit 2: School Brochures—Student Project Planner

Essential Question: How can students promote their school?

Project: Research your school. Use the information to create a brochure promoting the school. Place the finished brochure in a local real estate office; link your brochure to the office's website.

Steps

Step 1:   Review the "School Brochures Project Rubric" and "Project Self-Evaluation and Reflection" handouts.

Step 2:   Review the "What Is Informational Text?" handout.

Step 3:   Examine two brochures and complete the "Investigating Brochures" handout.

Step 4:   Review the "Tri-fold Brochure" and "Creating an Effective Informational Brochure" handouts.

Step 5:   Conduct school research and complete the "School Research" handout.

Step 6:   Create a rough draft of your brochure using the "Brochure Template" handout.

Step 7:   Use your completed "School Research" handout to create your brochure. There are several options for creating the brochure. Use a computer program such as Microsoft Word or an online brochure maker such as the one found at the URL address below. Consult with your teacher for guidelines.

   URL: <https://www.canva.com/create/brochures/>

Step 8:   Share your brochure with a local real estate office and the central school office. Post brochures on the classroom or school web page and/or linked to a local real estate office. Print copies may also be shared with a local real estate office and your central school office.

Step 9:   Complete the "Project Self-Evaluation and Reflection" handout.

Unit 2: School Brochures—What Is Informational Text?

Informational text is nonfiction writing written to convey factual information. This type of text can give you a lot of important information about people, places, and things.

When reading informational text, you should look at how the information is presented. Has the author used text features, such as illustrations or boldface print to emphasize key points? Understanding the purpose of text features will help you identify what is most important in the text.

Brochures, cookbooks, and newspapers are examples of informational text.

Text Features		
Print	**Definition**	**Purpose**
title	the name of the text	helps identify the topic of the text
heading	a name given to a section of text	helps identify main ideas of the section of text
boldface print	a word or phrase that is in darker print	signals the word is important
italicized print	a style of printing where letters slant to the right	draws attention to an extra-important idea
underlining	a line drawn under the text	signals the word, phrase, or idea is important
font	the type, size, and style of the text	draws the reader's attention to the text
bullet	a centered dot	emphasizes a list of items
asterisk	a small star-like symbol	indicates additional information is printed at the bottom of the page
caption	the words, phrase, or sentence(s) under or beside a photo or illustration	explains what is shown in an illustration/photograph
Graphic	**Definition**	**Purpose**
illustration/ photograph	a drawing or picture	shows instead of tells
sidebars	extra text in a section of the page that gives short information on the topic	highlights main text
map	a depiction of all or part of the earth drawn on a flat surface at a specific scale	signals location and shows a variety of information about a place
charts/tables	an organized picture of information or data	expands meaning of text
time line	a horizontal or vertical line marked chronologically with events	linear understanding of text
diagram	drawing or plan	explains by outlining parts and their relationships

Name: _____ Date: _____

Unit 2: School Brochures—Investigating Brochures

Directions: Select two brochures. Then complete the graphic organizer.

Brochure 1	Brochure 2
Title:	Title:
What is the brochure advertising?	What is the brochure advertising?
Who is the intended audience?	Who is the intended audience?
How does the cover contribute to the understanding of the information contained in the brochure?	How does the cover contribute to the understanding of the information contained in the brochure?
Check each print feature found in the brochure. _____ titles _____ headings _____ boldface print _____ italicized print _____ bullets _____ captions	Check each print feature found in the brochure. _____ titles _____ headings _____ boldface print _____ italicized print _____ bullets _____ captions
Check each graphic feature found in the brochure. _____ photograph/illustration _____ sidebar _____ map/chart/table _____ time line _____ diagram	Check each graphic feature found in the brochure. _____ photograph/illustration _____ sidebar _____ map/chart/table _____ time line _____ diagram

Unit 2: School Brochures—Tri-fold Brochure

> A **brochure** is a small booklet (often used for advertising) that contains information about an event, organization, institution, location, or product. Brochures come in a variety of designs, sizes, and formats.

Tri-fold Brochure

The tri-fold brochure is a single sheet of paper printed on both sides and folded into thirds.

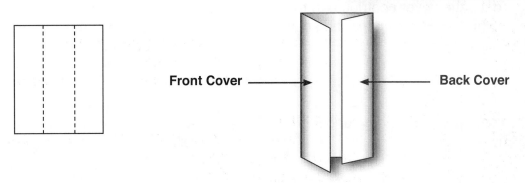

Front Cover → ← Back Cover

After folding, there are six panels for information (three panels on the outside and three panels on the inside).

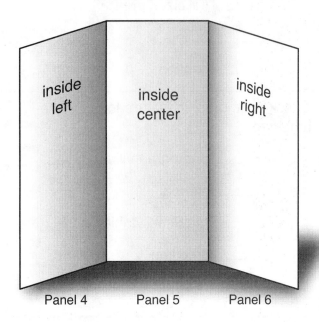

Outside Brochure

inside flap	outside center	front cover
Panel 3	Panel 2	Panel 1

Inside Brochure

inside left	inside center	inside right
Panel 4	Panel 5	Panel 6

Unit 2: School Brochures—
Creating an Effective Informational Brochure

Brochures target a specific audience, have a clear purpose, and answer the 5Ws: *who, what, where, when,* and *why.*

Checklist for an Effective Brochure

Cover
A good cover grabs the reader's attention and shows what information the brochure contains. The cover includes:
- a title that clearly identifies the topic.
- a graphic feature that relates to the topic.

Content
The text is nonfiction and written to covey factual information. The author
- uses descriptive and precise language.
- uses correct grammar, punctuation, spelling, and capitalization.

Introductory Information
The introduction or introductory paragraph is the most important part of an informational brochure. The paragraph:
- familiarizes the readers with the topic.
- provides basic background information and why the topic is important.

Details
Details provide more in-depth information about the topic. These details can be organized by using:
- headings–then write details under them.
- questions–ask an important question about the topic, then answer the question.

Print Features
A variety of print features are used to:
- help the reader more easily navigate the text.
- provide additional information to help the reader understand the content.

Graphic Features
Graphics support the information presented in the brochure. If using an online graphic, remember to include bibliographic information. This information can be placed:
- in a line underneath the graphic, saying where you got it and who it belongs to.
- under a bibliography heading on the last panel of the brochure.

Name: _____ Date: _____

Unit 2: School Brochures—School Research

Directions: Research your school to find the following information.

Complete school name: _____

Mascot: _____

Logo: _____

Address: _____

Superintendent's contact information: _____

_____

Middle School Office phone number: _____

Web site address: _____

School hours: _____

Mission or vision statement: _____

_____

_____

Educational opportunities (programs, clubs, teams etc.): _____

_____

_____

_____

Brief school history: _____

_____

_____

_____

Name: _____ Date: _____

Unit 2: School Brochures—School Research (cont.)

Calendar of school dates, vacations, and special events for the current school year:

August	September	October
November	December	January
February	March	April
May	June	July

Other important dates (summer programs, extended learning opportunities, etc.)

Current enrollment numbers:

Total _____   By grade level _____

_____

Names of school board members:

_____   _____

_____   _____

_____   _____

_____   _____

Unit 2: School Brochures—Brochure Template

A **template** is a pattern or model used as a guide to make something.

Directions: Follow the steps below to create a rough draft of your tri-fold brochure.

Step 1: Place a sheet of copy paper in landscape (horizontal) position on your desk. Fold the sheet into thirds. Unfold your paper.

Step 2: Use your completed "School Research" handout and the templates below to help you sketch a rough draft of your brochure.

Step 3: Leave a fourth-inch margin on all sides of the paper. Leave a half-inch gutter space between panels to allow for folding. Do not place any text or graphics in the gutter space.

Outside

(Inside Flap)	(Outside Center)	(Front Cover)
Calendar of school dates and events for the current school year	Basic information such as the school address, telephone numbers, school hours, names of the principals, superintendent, and board members	Name of your school and a picture of the school, school mascot, or school symbol

Tips

1. Use no more than two or three different fonts in your brochure.

2. Keep the number of colors used to a minimum.

3. Keep graphics and font in proportion.

4. Use headings and subheadings to divide chunks of information.

5. Keep the amount of information you place in each panel to a minimum.

Inside

(Inside Left)	(Inside Center)	(Inside Right)
Highlights of educational opportunities and programs that your school provides for students	Motto, mission, values, and goals	School's history

Unit 3: Red Wigglers—Teacher Information

Project Overview
Students will research vermicomposting. They will use the information to write an argumentative essay supporting the use of earthworms (red wrigglers) to recycle cafeteria food waste. They will gain permission for the project from the school administration. They will design, construct, and maintain a vermicomposting system.

Project Objectives
When students complete this project, they will be able to • use the Internet to research a topic. • create source cards and use to write a bibliography. • create note cards and use to write an argumentative essay. • collaborate with peers to design, construct, and maintain a vermicomposting system.

Integration of Academic Skills
• Language Arts: write a narrative • Science: design and construct a vermicomposting system • Technology: use computer word processing, graphic programs, online resources

Primary Common Core State Standards Addressed

ELA-Literacy.W.6.1 Write arguments to support claims with clear reasons and relevant evidence. ELA-Literacy.RST.6-8.3 Follow precisely a multistep procedure when carrying out experiments, taking measurements, or performing technical tasks.	ELA-Literacy.W.7.1 Write arguments to support claims with clear reasons and relevant evidence. ELA-Literacy.RST.6-8.3 Follow precisely a multistep procedure when carrying out experiments, taking measurements, or performing technical tasks.	ELA-Literacy.W.8.1 Write arguments to support claims with clear reasons and relevant evidence ELA-Literacy.RST.6-8.3 Follow precisely a multistep procedure when carrying out experiments, taking measurements, or performing technical tasks.

© Copyright 2010. National Governors Association Center for Best Practices and Council of Chief State School Officers. All rights reserved.

Essential Question	Type of Project
Can vermicomposting help reduce the amount of cafeteria food waste going to the local disposal facility?	☐ Individual Student ■ Collaborative Teams ■ Whole Class

Introductory Event
This unit is designed to be a collaborate project between the Language Arts and Science teachers. (Before getting started, contact your local health department concerning restrictions or guidelines for such a project.) 1. *Scenario:* Every school year, tons of cafeteria food waste is scraped into the garbage. The garbage must be picked up and transported to a disposal facility. Reducing the amount of solid waste going to the facility will save the school money and help the environment. 2. *Discussion:* Ask students to define vermicomposting. Record ideas. Provide the definition so students can compare with their ideas. (Vermicomposting is a system that uses red worms to process/eat kitchen waste.) 3. *Brainstorm:* Create a list of questions students have about vermicomposting. 4. *Guest Speaker:* Invite a specialist from your local University's Department of Biological and Agricultural Engineering to speak on the subject of vermicomposting. 5. *Exploration:* Students observe a red worm by using a magnifying lens and recording observations, investigating how the worm moves and conducting experiments to determine whether red worms prefer light or dark.

Unit 3: Red Wigglers—Teacher Information

Materials/Resources Needed

1. A copy of all handouts for each student: There are several options—paper copy, scan and download handouts to be used on a whiteboard, or post handouts to the classroom web page to be downloaded by students to their laptops.
2. Red wigglers and magnifying lenses
3. Materials to construct worm bins (to be determined by student research)
4. Supplies to maintain vermicomposting system (to be determined by student research)

Technology

1. Computers with word processing, printer, and graphic programs
2. Computers with Internet connections

Internet Tools for Accessing Information

The following websites offer teachers excellent information concerning setting up and maintaining a vermicomposting system as a classroom project.

The Worm Guide: a Vermicomposting Guide for Teachers
URL:<http://www.calrecycle.ca.gov/publications/Documents/Schools/56001007.pdf>

Leader's Guide (4-H) Vermicomposting
URL:<https://www.bae.ncsu.edu/topic/vermicomposting/pubs/ag-464-vermi-curriculum.pdf>

Managing the Project

Step 1: Launch Project–Discuss the essential question and complete the introductory activities.
Step 2: Review–"Red Wigglers Project Rubric" handout and "Project Self-Evaluation and Reflections" handout (page 6)
Step 3: Review–"Project Planner" handout
Step 4: Mini-Lesson–"Annelids" and "Vermicomposting" handouts
Step 5: Mini-Lesson–"What Is an Argumentative Essay?", "Pros and Cons", and "Argumentative Essay Planner" handouts
Step 6: Mini-Lesson–"Source Card vs. Note Card" and "Citing Sources" handouts (pages 40–42)
Step 7: Activity–Students conduct research. They create source cards to keep track of where they get information and note cards to record relevant information they plan to use in their news article.
Step 8: Review–Students review "The Writing Process" handout (page 53).
Step 9: Activity–Students organize their note cards and use to complete the "Argumentative Essay Planner."
Step 10: Activity–Students use their completed "Argumentative Essay Planner" handout to write their argumentative essay. Students proof and edit writing before submitting final copy.
Step 11: Activity–Students present project proposal, based on their argumentative essay, to school administration.
Step 12: Activity–Once administrators grant permission for the project, students design, construct, and maintain the vermicomposting system.
Step 13: Activity–Students harvest worms and bag compost to donate or sell to the community.

Project Evaluation

1. The teacher completes the "Red Wigglers Project Rubric" handout for each student.
2. Students complete "Project Self-Evaluation and Reflection" handout (page 6).
3. Teacher/student conferences are held to discuss the completed evaluations.

Name: _____ Date: _____

Red Wigglers Project Rubric

Argumentative Essay	Advanced	Proficient	Nearing Proficient	Below Proficient
Organization Introduces claims clearly and supports them with relevant evidence. Acknowledges opposing claims. Develops the topic with relevant facts and evidence. Provides a conclusion that follows format for argumentative essay. Uses appropriate transition words to make essay flow. Uses correct grammar, capitalization, punctuation, and spelling.	4	3	2	1
Content Thesis supported with relevant quotes, details, examples, and/or data. Information is appropriate, complete, factual, and accurate.	4	3	2	1
Research Uses relevant and credible sources. Cites sources accurately using correct format.	4	3	2	1
Project	Advanced	Proficient	Nearing Proficient	Below Proficient
Designs and constructs vermicomposting system, choosing resources appropriate for the purpose. Displays an understanding of earthworms and composting. Maintains vermicomposting system and care of earthworms.	4	3	2	1
Participation	Advanced	Proficient	Nearing Proficient	Below Proficient
Always positive attitude about the project, never critical of the project or the work of other team members. Consistently works to fulfill project requirements and perform individual team-member role.	4	3	2	1
Presentation	Advanced	Proficient	Nearing Proficient	Below Proficient
Presents a convincing argument for the project to school administration and parents. Covers topic completely and in depth. Includes essential information.	4	3	2	1

Teacher's comments:

Unit 3: Red Wigglers—Student Project Planner

Essential Question: Can vermicomposting help reduce the amount of cafeteria food waste going to the local disposal facility?

Project: Research vermicomposting. Use the information to write an argumentative essay supporting the use of earthworms to recycle school cafeteria waste. Share research with the school administration to gain permission for the project. Construct and maintain the vermicomposting system.

Steps

Step 1:   Review the "Red Wriggler Project Rubric" and "Project Self-Evaluation and Reflection" handouts.

Step 2:   Review the "Annelids" and "Vermicomposting" handouts. Formulate researchable questions. Begin by listing basic questions about your topic.

Step 3:   Review the "What Is an Argumentative Essay?" handout.

Step 4:   Review the "Source Card vs. Note Card" and "Citing Sources" handouts.

Step 5:   Locate and evaluate sources. For each source, record the bibliographic information on a separate index card. You will need this information for your bibliography. As you explore vermicomposting, consider both sides of the issue. Create note cards to record relevant evidence that supports your thesis. An excellent source with which to begin your research is the book *Worms Eat My Garbage* by Mary Appelhof. Next, go online to the URL addresses listed below.

URL: <http://compost.css.cornell.edu/worms/basics.html>
URL: <http://lancaster.unl.edu/pest/resources/vermicompost107.shtml>

Step 6:   Review the "The Writing Process" handout.

Step 7:   Organize your notes. Sort notes by subtopics. Evaluate each note for usefulness or need for further research. Arrange notes in a logical order for writing.

Step 8:   Use your note cards to complete the "Pros and Cons" and "Argumentative Essay Planner" handouts. Use the handouts to organize and compose your argumentative essay. Use your source cards and the "Citing Sources" handout to create your bibliography. Proof and edit your writing before submitting the final copy.

Step 9:   Share your research with the school administration to gain permission for the project.

Step 10:   Construct and maintain the vermicomposting system.

Step 11:   Complete the "Project Self-Evaluation and Reflection" handout.

Unit 3: Red Wigglers—Annelids

The most complex worms are the segmented worms, also called **annelids**. These worms have bodies with many segments, "ring-like sections," running from head to tail. There are approximately 9,000 species of annelids.

The best-known segmented worm is the earthworm, which lives in soil. They have a **coelom** [SEE lum]. A coelom is a liquid-filled space or body cavity that holds the internal organs. On the outside of their bodies they have **setae** [SEE tee] or bristle-like structures they use to burrow into the soil.

Earthworms are the most advanced worms. Redworms, commonly know as red wigglers, are a species of earthworm adapted to eating decaying organic material.They burrow in soil and live in moist areas. Earthworms have complex systems. They have blood vessels that carry food to all the cells. Because their blood remains inside vessels (a system of tubes), they have a closed circulatory system. If the blood moves through open spaces in an animal's body and does not flow through tubes, it has an open circulatory system. Earthworms also have a more advanced digestive system. They have a **crop** where the food is stored and a **gizzard** that grinds the food. The food is then digested in the intestines. Earthworms have a nervous system; nerves run along the body connecting to a simple brain at the **anterior** (front end). They have an excretory system of tubes that removes liquid waste from each segment. Earthworms lack a respiratory system, however. They exchange gases by diffusion through their moist skin. Earthworms respond to light, temperature, and moisture. Earthworms tunnel through the earth and loosen the soil, which lets air reach plant roots, and their waste material adds nutrients to the soil. They are often called the "farmer's friend."

Parts of an Earthworm

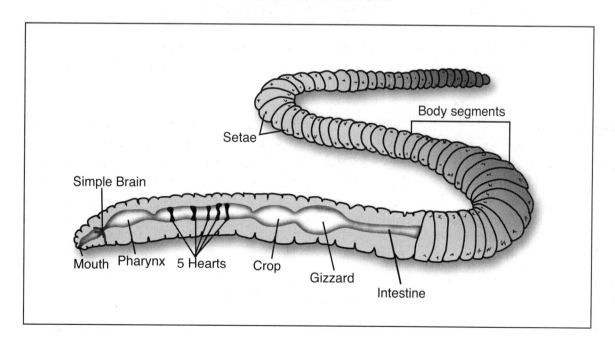

Unit 3: Red Wigglers—Vermicomposting

> **Vermicomposting** is a system that uses earthworms to recycle kitchen waste. During this process, the worms produce worm castings (waste) that are rich in nutrients and can be used as fertilizer for plants. The offspring produced during this process can be used by gardeners and fishermen.

The vermicomposting system is basically a worm farm. There are several questions to consider before starting your own system.

What materials and supplies will I need?

- Wooden box or plastic container with holes in bottom
- Bedding such as shredded cardboard or newsprint paper, decomposed leaves, and/or peat moss
- Water
- Biodegradable kitchen waste
- Redworms
- Black sheet of plastic slightly smaller than the worm bed surface to be placed on top of bed to retain moisture and keep out light.

What do worms need?

1. Temperature: your compost worms can tolerate a wide range of temperatures; however, they fair best in temperatures between 55–75° F.
2. Moisture: A worm's body consists of about 75% water; therefore, the bedding should have approximately the same moisture content. Water to bedding ratio = 3:1. This means add 3 pounds of water to every 1 pound of bedding.
3. Ventilation: Air must be able to circulate around your worm bin.
4. Food: earthworms should be fed biodegradable kitchen/cafeteria waste. The worm to garbage ratio = 2:1. This means for every 2 pounds of worms, you will need 1 pound of garbage each day.

Where do I get my worms?

- You can order worms from a local supplier, or you can order them on the Internet.
- Don't use night crawlers that live in the soil by your home to populate your compost bin. Night crawlers need to tunnel through dirt to eat and survive, and they can't live on vegetable waste. Instead, you need redworms—*Eisenia foetida* (red wiggler) and *Lumbricus rubellus* (manure worm).

When do I harvest my worms?

Every two to three months, harvest extra worms and change the bedding. The extra worms can then be sold to fishermen, bait shops, and gardeners or donated to your local community garden association.

Unit 3: Red Wigglers—What Is an Argumentative Essay?

An **argumentative essay**, also called a **persuasive essay**, is an essay in which the writer argues on a topic he or she has strong beliefs about.

In an argumentative essay, the writer makes a claim and supports it with evidence in order to convince or persuade the audience to agree. This type of essay includes three parts: introduction, body, and conclusion. For an argumentative essay to be effective, each part must contain certain elements. The first paragraph should include a brief explanation of your topic, background information, and claim or thesis statement. The thesis statement is your position on the topic. The three paragraphs of the body contain information that supports the claim with evidence and acknowledges opposing viewpoints. The conclusion restates your position.

Characteristics of an Argumentative/Persuasive Essay
- a clear statement of the writer's position, what he/she wants the reader to believe
- at least three strong reasons that support the argument
- elaboration of each argument with facts and examples
- convincing language that is both positive and polite
- clear organization that best persuades the reader
- a summarization of the argument and reasons at the end of the essay

Tips for Writing an Argumentative/Persuasive Essay
1. Write a clear, interesting, strong introduction to your essay.
   - Begin with a question to get your readers thinking; or
   - Begin with stating a fact to surprise your readers.
2. Use persuasive, positive language (e.g., *obviously, clearly, definitely,* etc.).
3. Avoid negative, loaded language and name-calling (*crazy, ridiculous, idiotic,* etc.).
4. Write a strong, forceful conclusion that briefly reviews your reasons.
5. Improve your essay by editing and proofing your work.

Effective Use of Transitional Words
Transitional words or phrases show logical connections between details. Using clear transitions helps show how your ideas relate to each other. Transitions are used to smoothly flow from one paragraph to the next in an essay.

Time or Sequence	Spatial	Compare	Contrast
first, second, then, next, later, soon, before, afterward, meanwhile	*in front of, behind, along, below, above, on the left, in the middle*	*similarly, likewise, also, like, as, nor, neither, either*	*yet, but, than, unlike, instead, whereas, while, however, otherwise*
Cause and Effect	**Degree of Importance**	**Adding Information**	**Summaries or Conclusions**
since, because, thus, so, therefore, due to, as a result, for this reason	*mainly, strongest, weakest, worst, best, most importantly*	*for example, again, also, another, besides, next, along with, finally*	*in conclusion, finally, therefore, in summary, as a result*

Name: _____ Date: _____

Unit 3: Red Wigglers—Pros and Cons

Directions: As you explore the question below, consider both sides of the issue. List arguments for (pros) and against (cons) the issue in the boxes. Then write your thesis statement.

> **Question:** Is vermicomposting a solution for reducing the amount of school waste that goes to the local disposal facility?

Pros (arguments for the issue)	Cons (arguments against the issue)
Claim #1: Fact or example: Source:	Counter Argument #1: Fact or example: Source:
Claim #2: Fact or example: Source:	Counter Argument #2: Fact or example: Source:
Claim #3: Fact or example: Source:	Counter Argument #3: Fact or example: Source:

Thesis statement: (Write a sentence that states your position on the issue. This is a request for change.)

Unit 3: Red Wigglers—Argumentative Essay Planner

Paragraph #1–Introduction

Topic: _____

Opponents believe _____

Proponents argue _____

Thesis Statement: (Your opinion and why) _____

Paragraph #2–Claim
Claim #1: (Why someone should agree with your opinion.)

Cite evidence and source:

Paragraph #3–Claim
Claim #2: (Why someone should agree with your opinion.)

Cite evidence and source:

Paragraph #4–Claim
Claim #3: (Why someone should agree with your opinion.)

Cite evidence and source:

Paragraph #5–Conclusion

Restate Opponent's view: _____

Restate Proponent's view: _____

Restate three reasons you agree: _____

State why your thesis statement is correct: _____

Unit 4: Virtual Museums—Teacher Information

Project Overview

Students will research their community's history. They will use the information to create a virtual museum.

Project Objectives

When students complete this project, they will be able to
- write a research report and cite sources correctly.
- collaborate with peers to create a virtual museum exhibit.

Integration of Academic Skills

- History/Social Studies: research
- Language Arts: write informational text
- Technology: use computer word processing, graphic programs, online resources

Primary Common Core State Standards Addressed

ELA-Literacy.RH.6-8.8 Distinguish among fact, opinion, and reasoned judgment in a text. ELA-Literacy.W.6.2 Write informative/explanatory texts to examine a topic and convey ideas, concepts, and information through the selection, organization, and analysis of relevant content. ELA-Literacy.W.6.6 Use technology, including the Internet, to produce and publish writing as well as to interact and collaborate with others; demonstrate sufficient command of keyboarding skills to type a minimum of three pages in a single sitting.	ELA-Literacy.RH.6-8.8 Distinguish among fact, opinion, and reasoned judgment in a text. ELA-Literacy.W.7.2 Write informative/explanatory texts to examine a topic and convey ideas, concepts, and information through the selection, organization, and analysis of relevant content. ELA-Literacy.W.7.6 Use technology, including the Internet, to produce and publish writing and link to and cite sources as well as to interact and collaborate with others, including linking to and citing sources.	ELA-Literacy.RH.6-8.8 Distinguish among fact, opinion, and reasoned judgment in a text. ELA-Literacy.W.8.2 Write informative/explanatory texts to examine a topic and convey ideas, concepts, and information through the selection, organization, and analysis of relevant content. ELA-Literacy.W.8.6 Use technology, including the Internet, to produce and publish writing and present the relationships between information and ideas efficiently as well as to interact and collaborate with others.

© Copyright 2010. National Governors Association Center for Best Practices and Council of Chief State School Officers. All rights reserved.

Essential Question	Type of Project
How can students help preserve the history of their community?	☐ Individual Student ■ Collaborative Teams ☐ Whole Class

Introductory Event

(This project provides an opportunity for collaboration between the Language Arts and Social Studies teachers and the local museum curator.)

1. *Scenario:* The Chamber of Commerce in your local community would like to share the history of the community using online exhibits. They would like you to create a virtual museum to provide information about how the community was founded, the stories of the people, historical sites, and artifacts that make the history of your community unique.
2. *Discussion:* As a class, discuss what students know about the history of their community. Generate a list of notable community history.
3. *Activity:* Go online to the Smithsonian National Museum of Natural History at <http://naturalhistory.si.edu/VT3>. Take one of the many virtual museum tours.
4. *Guest Speaker:* Invite a local historian to speak about the history of the community.

Unit 4: Virtual Museums—Teacher Information

Materials/Resources Needed
1. A copy of all handouts for each student: There are several options—paper copy, scan and download handouts to be used on a whiteboard, or post handouts to the classroom web page to be downloaded by students to their laptops.

Technology
1. Computers with word processing, printer, and graphic programs
2. Computers with Internet connections

Internet Tools for Creating a Virtual Museum
The following sites offer tools for creating virtual museums.

URL: <http://christykeeler.com/EducationalVirtualMuseums.html>
Sample virtual museum rooms as well as a full template to create a virtual museum.

URL: <http://tool4learning.org/wp/mtp/2011/10/17/creating-virtual-museums/>
This site has helpful information on creating virtual museums using PowerPoint. A variety of free templates are provided for virtual museum rooms and full virtual museums.

URL: <https://www.youtube.com/watch?v=gT6lI8fZ8HI>
This site has information that will help students create source cards and note cards.

Managing the Project

Step 1: Launch Project–Discuss the essential question and complete introductory activities.
Step 2: Review–"Virtual Museums Project Rubric" handout and "Project Self-Evaluation and Reflection" handout (page 6)
Step 3: Review–"Student Project Planner" handout
Step 4: Mini-Lesson–"Museum Research Report" handout
Step 5: Mini-Lesson–"Source Card vs. Note Card" and "Citing Sources" handouts
Step 6: Mini-Lesson–"Writing an Outline" handout
Step 7: Mini-Lesson–"Creating a Virtual Museum" handout
Step 8: Activity–Students conduct community history research. They create source cards to keep track of where they get information and note cards to record relevant information they plan to use in their research report.
Step 9: Review–Students review "The Writing Process" handout (page 53).
Step 10: Activity–Students organize their note cards and create an outline using the "Writing an Outline" handout as a guide.
Step 11: Activity–Students use their outline to write a research report. They use their source cards to write a bibliography. Students proof and edit the work before submitting the final copy.
Step 12: Activity–Students complete the "Virtual Museums Planner" handout. They use the planner and an online museum template or a computer program such as Microsoft Word to create their virtual museums.
Step 13: Activity–Students share their project with the community. You may want to invite parents and community members to a celebration showcasing the virtual museum projects. You may also want to create a web page or classroom blog post with links to each team's project.

Project Evaluation

1. The teacher completes the "Virtual Museums Project Rubric" handout for each student.
2. Students complete the "Project Self-Evaluation and Reflection" handout (page 6).
3. Teacher/student conferences are held to discuss the completed evaluations.

Virtual Museums Project Rubric

Name: _____   Date: _____

Research Report

	Advanced	Proficient	Nearing Proficient	Below Proficient
Content: Fully understands the purpose for writing a research report. Topic developed with relevant facts and evidence. Information organized logically. It is interesting, accurate, complete, and factual.	4	3	2	1
Organization: Introductory paragraph interest-catching and tells the main idea. Other paragraphs well-organized with topic sentences for each new main idea. Transitional sentences lead from one main idea to the next. Written in the writer's own words, not copied from sources. Conclusion is a well-organized paragraph that sums up the research.	4	3	2	1
Research: Sources are relevant and credible. Bibliography is an accurate listing of all sources. Citations are correctly written.	4	3	2	1

Virtual Museum

	Advanced	Proficient	Nearing Proficient	Below Proficient
The exhibit is organized around an identifiable theme. It tells a "story" or conveys a message to the visitors. Key elements effectively tell different parts of the story. Artifacts include relevant primary sources, quotes, and/or facts that illustrate each part of the story.	4	3	2	1

Collaboration

	Advanced	Proficient	Nearing Proficient	Below Proficient
Uses time effectively in class and focuses on the virtual museum project. Always displays positive attitude about the project, never critical of the project or the work of other team members. Consistently works to fulfill project requirements and perform individual team-member role.	4	3	2	1

Teacher Comments:

Unit 4: Virtual Museums—Student Project Planner

Essential Question: How can students help preserve the history of their community?

Project: Research an important aspect of your community's local history. Use the research to write a research report. Then use your research report to create a virtual museum exhibit.

Steps

Step 1:   Review the "Virtual Museums Project Rubric" and "Project Self-Evaluation and Reflection" handouts.

Step 2:   Select a topic from the list of community history generated in the class discussion.

Step 3:   Review the "Museum Research Report" handout.

Step 4:   Review "Source Card vs. Note Card," "Citing Sources," and "Writing an Outline" handouts.

Step 5:   Locate and evaluate sources. Begin your research by looking for information about your topic online and in print sources. For each source, record the bibliography information on a separate index card. You will need this information for your bibliography. Write relevant information about your topic on your note cards.

Step 6:   Organize your note cards by subtopics. Evaluate each note for usefulness or need for further research. Arrange notes in a logical order for writing.

Step 7:   Create an outline from your organized note cards.

Step 8:   Use your outline to write your museum research report. Use your source cards and the "Citing Sources" handout to create your bibliography. Proof and edit your writing before submitting the final copy.

Step 9:   Plan your virtual museum by completing a "Virtual Museum Planner" handout for each room of your museum.

Step 10: Review the "Creating a Virtual Museum" handout to select an online template that is best for you and then create your museum.

Step 11: Share your virtual museum with members of your community. (See teacher for specifics.)

Step 12: Complete the "Project Self-Evaluation and Reflection" handout.

Unit 4: Virtual Museums—Museum Research Report

A **research report** presents information learned through research about a topic.

Research Report

The following steps will help you write your research report.

Step 1:   Select a historical figure or event from your community to research.

Step 2:   Make a K-W-L chart. Fill in the "What I know…" and "What I want to know…" sections. This will direct your research. Complete the "What I've learned…" section after researching your topic. This section can help you determine your outline headings.

K *What I know…*	W *What I want to know…*	L *What I've learned…*

Step 3:   Locate information about your topic. Use online and print sources.

Step 4:   Research your topic. Look for photographs, quotes, and facts that can be used to tell your museum exhibit story. Create note and source cards for the information you want to use in your report.

Step 5:   Make an outline from your note cards.

Step 6:   Use your outline to write your research report. Turn each main heading from your outline into a topic sentence. Write paragraphs from the subheadings and details from your outline.

Step 7:   Create a bibliography from your source cards.

Step 8:   Revise and edit your report.

Step 9:   Use your research report to create your virtual museum exhibit.

Characteristics of a Good Research Report

Content
- Topic: developed with relevant facts and evidence
- Information: organized logically. It is interesting, accurate, complete, and factual.

Organization
- Introductory paragraph: Interest-catching and tells the main idea
- Other paragraphs: well-organized with topic sentences for each new main idea
- Transitional sentences: lead from one main idea to the next
- Voice: written in the writer's own words, not copied from sources
- Summary/conclusion: well-organized paragraph that sums up the research

Research
- Sources: relevant and credible sources
- Bibliography: accurate listing of all sources
- Citations: correctly written

Unit 4: Virtual Museums—Creating a Virtual Museum

Virtual museums are organized collections of digitally recorded video segments, photographs, paintings, newspaper articles, historical data, and transcripts of interviews; basically, anything that can be digitized! Using a computer and the Internet, digitized representations can be brought together from multiple sources to be enjoyed and shared.

The purpose of your virtual museum is to preserve a collection of artifacts about your community. It should focus on an important aspect of your local history.

Your Museum Exhibit

Museum exhibits have a theme. The museum curator organizes the artifacts around the theme in order to tell a "story" or convey a message to the visitors. You will be the curator for your museum.

Think of your virtual museum as a building. As visitors enter they will find the name of the exhibit. They will explore "wings" of the building dedicated to key elements of the story you are telling. Each "wing" will have "rooms" featuring "displays" of artifacts that illustrate different parts of the story.

Planning Your Museum

- Story: Identify the story you want to tell.
- Theme: Determine the message of your story.
- Key Elements: Create a list of the parts of the story that you will present.
- Artifacts/Text: Use primary sources, quotes, and/or facts to illustrate each part of the story.
- Research: Gather the artifacts and resources needed to tell your story.

Virtual Museum Formats

There are several options for creating your virtual museum. Go online and investigate the websites below to determine which is best for you.

1. Educational Virtual Museums
   URL: <http://christykeeler.com/EducationalVirtualMuseums.html>

2. Microsoft PowerPoint (creating a virtual museum tutorial)
   URL: <https://www.youtube.com/watch?v=ed5e-HHikGk>

3. Creating Virtual Museums
   URL:<http://tool4learning.org/wp/mtp/2011/10/17/creating-virtual-museums>

Unit 4: Virtual Museums—Source Card vs. Note Card

> **Source cards** are a method of recording the bibliographic information for each source you have evaluated and are going to use.

Begin your research by looking for information about your topic in books, magazines, and online. Select information that applies directly to your topic and that comes from reputable and respected sources.

✔ Check the author's credentials. Is the author an expert on the topic? Has the author written other books or articles on the topic? Has the author been published in a respected publication or on a respected website?

✔ Check the publication date. Is this the most current information you can find on the topic?

✔ Check reliability of the source: If you have question about whether you are using a creditable source, ask your teacher or media center specialist.

Creating Source Cards

The source cards below were created by Lori for a research report on President Harry S Truman. For the first source used, she wrote the word "Source 1" in the upper right-hand corner of the index card. Next, Lori added the bibliographic information. Lori then continued researching Truman. With each new source used, she completed a new index card.

Book

Source 1

Author: Truman, Harry S

Title: <u>Collected Works of Harry S Truman</u>

City of Publication: New York

Publisher: Oak Tree Publishing **Date:** 2006

Call Number: 818 LIN

Location of Source: School Library

Encyclopedia

Source 2

Title of Entry: Truman, Harry S

Title of Encyclopedia: <u>World Book Encyclopedia</u>

Edition: 15th ed.

Date of Publication: 2013

Location of Source: School Library

Magazine

Source 3

Author: Armstrong, William

Title of Article: "Life of Harry S Truman"

Title of Magazine: <u>Cobblestone</u>

Date of Publication: Sept. 2014

Page Number: 45

Call Number: 3982 DAS 1993 4356

Location of Source: Public Library

Internet Address

Source 4

Author: Webster, Katherine

Title: "Harry S Truman"

URL: http://www.gov/presidents/harrystruman

Date of Access: Nov. 12, 2016

Date of Publication: 2013

Unit 4: Virtual Museums—Source Card vs. Note Card (cont.)

A **note card** is a record of the information you want to use in a research report. The information recorded on the card includes the title (topic) of the research, a source number (lets the researcher know from which source the information was taken), information to be used, identifies the note-taking method, and lists the page number(s) where the information can be found.

As you find information that you want to use in your research report, record each fact or detail on a separate index card. Three note-taking methods are listed below.

- Quoting: copying the author's exact wording or phrasing and enclosing it in quotation marks
- Paraphrasing: restating the main idea and supporting details of the passage in your own words
- Summarizing: rephrasing the main ideas of the passage

Creating Note Cards

Lori found information she wanted to use in her report about Harry S Truman in several sources. For each source she first created a source card, and then she created a note card to record the important fact or detail. She was careful to make sure that the number on each source card corresponded to a number on the correct note card to help her keep track from which source the fact or detail was taken.

Direct Quote

Topic: Truman	Source 1

"I realize the tragic significance of the atom bomb,"

(President Harry Truman in a radio address before the Japanese government finally surrendered in 1945.)

Quote	Page 220

Paraphrase

Topic: Truman	Source 2

Truman had no regrets because he thought he had made the right decision to drop the atomic bomb on Japan.

Paraphrase	Page 410

Summarize

Topic: Truman	Source 3

Truman had no regrets over his decision to drop the atom bomb on Japan during World War II. He believed it saved thousands of American and Japanese lives by quickly ending the war.

Summary	Page 25

Unit 4: Virtual Museums—Citing Sources

A **bibliography** is a list of all of the sources you have used in the process of researching a topic. The sources are compiled on a "Bibliography" or "Works Cited" page.

Citation Reminders

- Entry begins flush against the left margin
- Allow 1-inch margins
- Font size is 10 or 12 point
- Font type is Times New Roman or Arial
- Indent five spaces on the second line and all following lines that belong to the entry
- Punctuate titles
- Single space after punctuation marks
- Double space between entries

Correctly Writing a Citation

The hardest parts of writing a citation are figuring out which words should be capitalized, how to punctuate titles, and where to place the punctuation marks. Use the examples below as a guide for writing your bibliography.

Bibliography Entry Examples	
Audiovisual Materials "Title of Material." Type of material. Place of Publication; Publisher, Publication Date.	**Interview** Last name of person interviewed, First name of person interviewed. Type of Interview. Date.
Book Last name, First name. *Title of book.* Place of publication: Publisher, Publication Date.	**Magazine or Newspaper Article** Last name, First name. "Title or Headline of Article." *Name of Magazine or Newspaper.* Publication Date, Page Numbers.
CD-ROM "Title of Article." *Title of CD-ROM.* Medium Accessed. Volume number. Place of Publication: Publisher, Publication Date.	**Signed Encyclopedia Article** Last name, First name. "Title of Article." *Name of Encyclopedia.* Publication Date. Volume Number, Page Numbers.
Internet Website Last name, First name. "Title of Item." *Website Title.* Publisher of Website, Publication Date. Medium Accessed. Date Accessed. <electronic address>.	**Unsigned Encyclopedia Article** "Title of Article." *Name of Encyclopedia.* Publication Date. Volume Number, Page Numbers.
Photographs, Illustrations, and Drawings Creator's Last name, First name. *Title of Photograph.* Original Publication Date. *Title of Online Collection.* Date of Posting. Current Location of Original Document. Medium Accessed. Sponsoring Organization. Date Accessed. <electronic address>.	

Name: _____ Date: _____

Unit 4: Virtual Museums—Writing an Outline

An **outline** is a general plan for your writing. An outline shows the main topics, subtopics, and details that your paper will include. An outline uses sequence to help you organize ideas for a report or essay.
- Chronological order tells the order in which events happened.
- Spatial order describes the location of things in a place.
- Logically order groups of related ideas, such as details, in order of importance.

Directions: Review the following outline of the events in the life of President Harry S Truman. Notice how the main headings and subheadings are arranged by time sequence when doing biographical research. Then, underline the title; highlight Roman numerals (main topics) in yellow, and capital letters (subtopics) in green.

Harry S Truman

I. Childhood
   A. Born May 8, 1884
   B. Born in Lamar, Missouri
   C. Grew up in Independence, MO
II. Family
   A. Parents, John and Martha (Young) Truman
   B. Brother, Vivian
   C. Sister, Mary Jane
III. Education
   A. Attended public schools in Independence, MO
   B. Graduated from Independence High School in 1901
IV. Achievements
   A. Served in the Missouri National Guard from 1905 to 1911
   B. Elected presiding judge in the Jackson County Court in 1926 and 1930
   C. Elected to the United States Senate in 1934
   D. Elected vice president with Franklin Roosevelt in 1944
   E. Became America's 33rd president April 12, 1945

Guidelines for Outlining

1. Write the title of your research paper at the top of the page. Use capital letters to begin the first, last, and all important words.
2. Use Roman numerals for main topics and capital letters for subtopics. Place a period after each Roman numeral and capital letter.

Roman Numerals

$I = 1$
$II = 2$
$III = 3$
$IV = 4$
$V = 5$
$VI = 6$
$VII = 7$
$VIII = 8$
$IX = 9$
$X = 10$

3. Begin the first word in each main topic and subtopic with a capital letter.
4. Indent the subtopics evenly.

Name: _____   Date: _____

Unit 4: Virtual Museums—Virtual Museum Planner

Directions: Use the graphic organizer to plan one room of your virtual museum. Complete a copy of this page for each room of your exhibit.

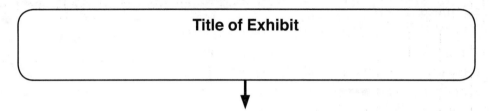

Title of Exhibit

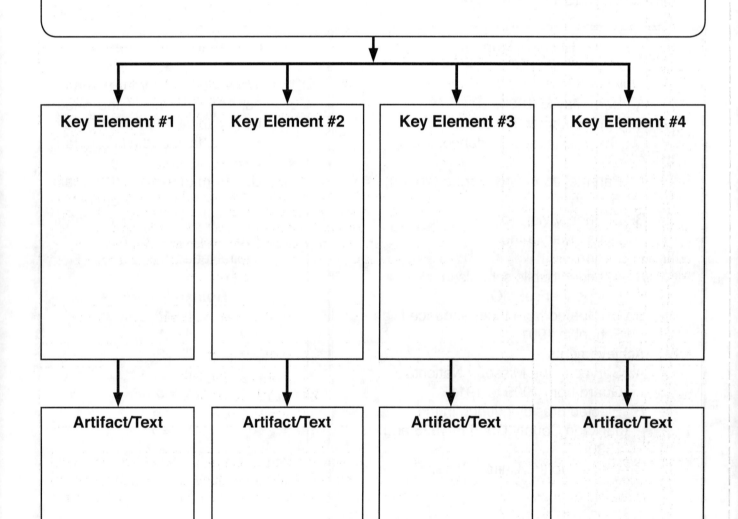

Theme: (The message that you want your visitors to take away from your exhibit in this room.)

Key Element #1	Key Element #2	Key Element #3	Key Element #4

Artifact/Text	Artifact/Text	Artifact/Text	Artifact/Text

Unit 5: Calories Count—Teacher Information

Project Overview

Students will research the *Healthy Hunger-Free Kids Act* and dietary requirements for teens. They will use the information to write a news article promoting healthy food choices. The articles and weekly nutritional information for the school lunch menu will be shared with students and the community through the classroom web page, blog, or school website.

Project Objectives

When students complete this project, they will be able to
- use the Internet to research a topic.
- create source cards and write a bibliography.
- use technology to produce and publish a news article.
- collaborate with peers.

Integration of Academic Skills

- Math: Compute fluently with multi-digit numbers
- Language Arts: write informational text
- Technology: use computer word processing, graphic programs, online resources

Primary Common Core State Standards Addressed

ELA-Literacy.W.6.2 Write informative/explanatory texts to examine a topic and convey ideas, concepts, and information through the selection, organization, and analysis of relevant content.	ELA-Literacy.W.7.2 Write informative/explanatory texts to examine a topic and convey ideas, concepts, and information through the selection, organization, and analysis of relevant content.	ELA-Literacy.W.8.2 Write informative/explanatory texts to examine a topic and convey ideas, concepts, and information through the selection, organization, and analysis of relevant content.
ELA-Literacy.W.6.6 Use technology, including the Internet, to produce and publish writing as well as to interact and collaborate with others; demonstrate sufficient command of keyboarding skills to type a minimum of three pages in a single sitting.	ELA-Literacy.W.7.6 Use technology, including the Internet, to produce and publish writing and link to and cite sources as well as to interact and collaborate with others, including linking to and citing sources.	ELA-Literacy.W.8.6 Use technology, including the Internet, to produce and publish writing and present the relationships between information and ideas efficiently as well as to interact and collaborate with others.

© Copyright 2010. National Governors Association Center for Best Practices and Council of Chief State School Officers. All rights reserved.

Essential Question	Type of Project
How can students be encouraged to make healthy food choices in the school cafeteria?	☐ Individual Student ■ Collaborative Teams ☐ Whole Class

Introductory Event

(This project provides an opportunity for collaboration between the Language Arts and Math teachers.)
1. *Scenario:* According to the United States Department of Agriculture, about one-third of teens are overweight or obese. Realizing this problem could affect students at our middle school, parents and faculty want to encourage healthy eating habits.
2. *Discussion:* Lunch is an essential part of a balanced diet. As a class, discuss the benefits of eating a healthy lunch each day. Ask students which foods they typically eat in the cafeteria and which ones they typically avoid.
3. *Activity:* Students examine the monthly school lunch menu. Note the types of foods offered.
4. *Guest Speaker:* Invite the school dietitian to speak about the school lunch program.

Unit 5: Calories Count—Teacher Information

Materials/Resources Needed
1. A copy of all handouts for each student: There are several options—paper copy, scan and download handouts to be used on a whiteboard, or post handouts to the classroom web page to be downloaded by students to their laptops.

Technology
1. Computers with word processing, printer, and graphic programs
2. Computers with Internet connections

Internet Tools for Creating a News Article
The following sites offer tools and helpful information for creating news articles:
URL: <http://www.extranewspapers.com/newspaper-template-pack-word-school> This site has a variety of free templates for creating a news article. It requires the file to be downloaded to a computer.
URL: <https://www.youtube.com/watch?v=FZvgbUoDkYU> This site demonstrates the use of the inverted pyramid for writing a news article.

Managing the Project
Step 1: Launch Introductory Event–Present the essential question and complete introductory activities.
Step 2: Review–"Calories Count Project Rubric" handout and "Project Self-Evaluation and Reflection" handout (page 6)
Step 3: Review–"Student Project Planner" handout
Step 4: Mini-Lesson–"Promoting Good Health" handout
Step 5: Mini-Lesson–"Informative/Explanatory Writing", "Elements of a News Article", and "The Writing Process" handouts
Step 6: Mini-Lesson–"Source Card vs. Note Card" and "Citing Sources" handouts (pages 40–42)
Step 7: Activity–Students conduct research. They create source cards to keep track of where they get information and note cards to record relevant information they plan to use in their news article.
Step 8: Review–Students review "The Writing Process" handout.
Step 9: Activity–Students organize their note cards and create an outline using the "News Article Outline" handout.
Step 10: Activity–Students use the completed "News Article Outline" handout to write their news article. Students proof and edit their work before publishing. There are several options for formatting the news article. Students may use a computer program such as Microsoft Word or an online news article template.
Step 11: Activity–Students share their project with students and the community. You may want to create a web page or classroom blog post with links to each team's project or post on the school website.

Project Evaluation
1. The teacher completes the "Calories Count Project Rubric" handout for each student.
2. Students complete the "Project Self-Evaluation and Reflection" handout (page 6).
3. Teacher/student conferences are held to discuss the completed evaluations.

Name: _____ Date: _____

Calories Count Project Rubric

Component	Criteria	Score
News Article	Article has a headline that captures the reader's attention and accurately describes the content. Lead paragraph reveals all the important information and answers the *who, what, when, where, why,* and *how* of the story. Explanation paragraphs contain quotes, supporting details, examples, and/or data. The conclusion wraps up the article. Writer demonstrates command of conventions; correct grammar and rules for capitalization, punctuation, and spelling.	4 Excellent 3 Acceptable 2 Average 1 Needs Work
Research	Uses relevant and credible sources. Cites source accurately using correct format.	4 Excellent 3 Acceptable 2 Average 1 Needs Work
Project	The project is well thought out. Effectively uses appropriate communication tools to convey the project message (posted on wiki, blog, or school website as directed by teacher). Layout displays creativity and originality including pictures, graphics, or other visual aids. The font is readable and does not detract from the content.	4 Excellent 3 Acceptable 2 Average 1 Needs Work
Participation	Uses time wisely in class and focuses on the project. Always positive attitude about the project, never critical of the project or the work of other team members. Consistently works to fulfill project requirements and perform individual team-member responsibility.	4 Excellent 3 Acceptable 2 Average 1 Needs Work

Teacher Comments:

Unit 5: Calories Count—Student Project Planner

Essential Question: How can students be encouraged to make healthy food choices in the school cafeteria?

Project: Research the *Healthy Hunger-Free Kids Act* and dietary requirements for teens. Use the information to write a news article promoting healthy food choices. Share the article and weekly nutritional information for the school lunch menu with students and the community through the classroom web page, blog, or school website.

Steps

Step 1:   Review the "Calories Count Project Rubric" and "Project Self-Evaluation and Reflection" handouts.

Step 2:   Review the "Promoting Good Health" handout. Formulate researchable questions. Begin by listing basic questions you have about teen nutritional needs.

Step 3:   Review the "Informative/Explanatory Writing" and "Elements of a News Article" handouts.

Step 4:   Review the "Source Card vs. Note Card" and "Citing Sources" handouts.

Step 5:   Conduct your research. Locate and evaluate sources. For each source, record the bibliographic information on a separate index card. You will need this information for your bibliography. Create note cards for relevant information you plan to use in your article.

Step 6:   Review the "The Writing Process" handout.

Step 7:   Organize your notes. Evaluate each note for usefulness or need for further research. Arrange notes in a logical order for writing.

Step 8:   Use your note cards to complete the "News Article Outline" handout. Then use the outline to organize and compose your news article. There are several options for formatting your article. Use a computer program such as Microsoft Word or an online news article template. (Consult your teacher for instructions.)

Step 9:   Use your source cards and the "Citing Sources" handout to create your bibliography. Proof and edit your article and bibliography before submitting the final copy.

Step 10:   Work with your school dietitian to compile nutritional information and calorie count for the foods offered through the school's daily lunch program.

Step 11:   Share your completed project with students and community by uploading or linking it to the classroom web page, blog, or school website. (Consult your teacher for instructions.)

Step 12:   Update the nutritional information and calorie count for lunch menus as needed throughout the school year. (Consult your teacher for instructions.)

Step 13:   Complete the "Project Self-Evaluation and Reflection" handout.

Unit 5: Calories Count—Promoting Healthy Eating

> The energy in food is measured in **calories**.

You smile at a friend. You shoot baskets after school. Both of these activities use energy. Your body gets the energy from food. Foods that contain starch, sugar, protein, and fat have calories. Fatty foods contain the most calories.

Daily Calorie Count

How many calories a day does your body need to stay healthy? Consuming adequate calories from nutritious foods is important for proper growth and development. The United States Department of Agriculture (USDA) has determined the number of daily calories required by middle-school students between the ages of 9 and 12.

Number of Calories Needed Each Day	
Middle-School Boys	**Middle-School Girls**
Sedentary: 1,600 to 2,000	Sedentary: 1,400 to 1,600
Moderately Active: 1,800 to 2,200	Moderately Active: 1,600 to 2,000
Active: 2,000 to 2,800	Active: 1,800 to 2,200

Promoting Good Health Habits

According to the USDA, about one-third of teens are overweight or obese. In 2010, Congress passed the *Healthy Hunger-free Kids Act* to fight childhood obesity and promote health. The law set mandatory guidelines for school lunch programs receiving federal lunch aid. It requires school cafeterias to serve more fruits and vegetables and to limit the amounts of proteins and carbohydrates served. One of the biggest changes taking place is the introduction of meal calorie limits. School lunches must not exceed 700 calories for grades 6–8.

Unit 5: Calories Count—Informative/Explanatory Writing

Informative writing is also known as **explanatory** or **expository writing**. This form of writing explains a topic by presenting facts, quotations, and other evidence about the topic. It can be used to explain the importance of a healthy diet, to explore the causes of school bullying, or to compare two pieces of literature. Your goal is to give an objective, fair view of the topic. A newspaper article is a good example of informative writing. There are several forms of informative writing, such as cause/effect, compare/contrast, description, and problem/solution.

Forms of Informative/Explanatory Writing

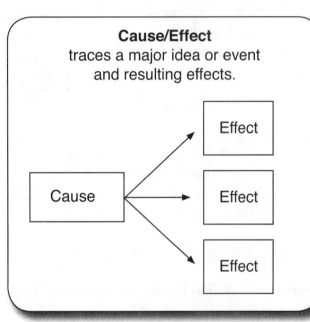

Cause/Effect
traces a major idea or event and resulting effects.

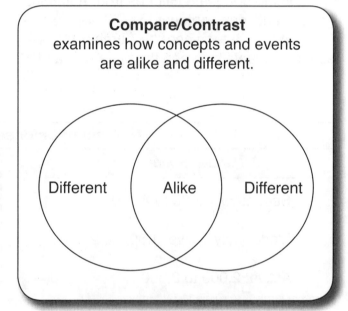

Compare/Contrast
examines how concepts and events are alike and different.

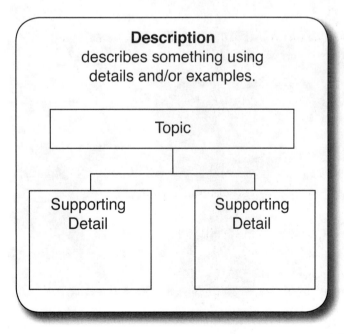

Description
describes something using details and/or examples.

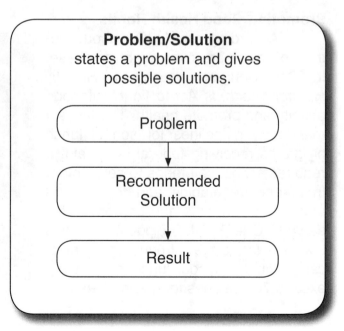

Problem/Solution
states a problem and gives possible solutions.

Unit 5: Calories Count—Elements of a News Article

> The purpose of a **news article** is to inform readers of facts and information about current or recent events. News articles contain factual information rather than personal opinions or slanted comments.

Five Parts of a News Article

There are certain elements that are common to almost all news articles.

- **Headline:** A short attention-getting phrase that presents the main idea of the article
- **Byline:** Tells who wrote the story
- **Lead Paragraph (Introduction):** All the important information is revealed in the opening paragraph. It contains the answers to the *who, what, when, where, why,* and *how* of the news story.
- **Explanation:** This section includes paragraphs containing supporting details that give a more complete picture of the event.
- **Conclusion:** A paragraph that wraps up the article

Helpful Hints

1. Tell the story in a way that holds the reader's interest.
2. Make the story stick in the minds of the readers by writing a dynamite conclusion.
3. Use text features and graphics to enhance the reader's understanding of information presented.

Inverted Pyramid

It is helpful to picture an upside-down pyramid when writing a newspaper article.

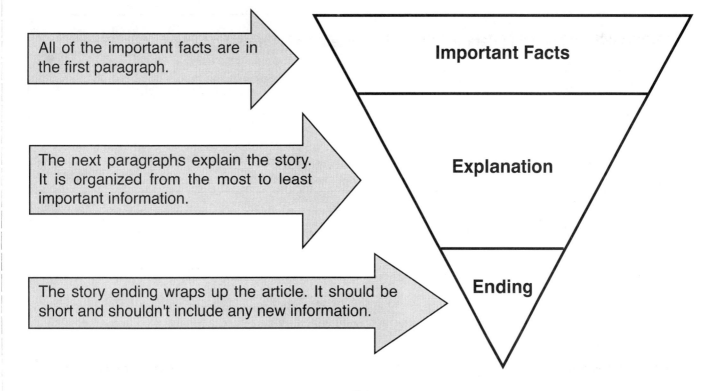

All of the important facts are in the first paragraph. → **Important Facts**

The next paragraphs explain the story. It is organized from the most to least important information. → **Explanation**

The story ending wraps up the article. It should be short and shouldn't include any new information. → **Ending**

Name: _____   Date: _____

Unit 5: Calories Count—News Article Outline

Directions: Use your research to fill in the outline with the information you will be including in your news article.

Headline: _____

Byline: (your name) _____

Lead Paragraph

    Who: _____

    What: _____

    When: _____

    Where: _____

    Why: _____

    How: _____

Explanation: (supporting details, quotes, examples, and interesting facts)

Conclusions: (wraps up the article and makes the story stick in the mind of the reader)

Unit 5: Calories Count—The Writing Process

WRITING PLAN	**After researching your topic...** • Organize your note cards. Sort cards by subtopics: description of problem, recommended solution, explanation of solution, and conclusion. Read all the notes in each subtopic, and put the cards in a logical order. Discard all note cards that are not usable or duplicate information on another card. • Create a writing plan. An outline is one type of writing plan. It shows the topics and subtopics that your paper will include.

DRAFT	**Write the first draft.** • The purpose of writing the first draft is to put your ideas down on paper. Follow your writing plan, adding in details. If you cannot think of the best way to say something, write it down as well as you can and keep on writing. • Develop a thesis statement by focusing on the writing prompt. • Write in sentences and paragraphs. Use your own language.

REVISE	**Re-read draft and decide what works. Ask these questions.** • Do I need to add or delete details? • Did I use a variety of sentence structures? • Did I make clear transitions between sentences and between paragraphs? • Did I use the appropriate word choice for my audience and purpose?

EDIT	**Proofread and correct errors.** • Grammar: Check for misuse in verb forms, possessive and plural nouns, homophones and homographs, and person. • Punctuation: Check for correct use of commas, semicolons, and colons. Check each sentence for correct ending punctuation. • Capitalization: Check for capitals at the beginning of each sentence and capitalization of proper nouns and proper adjectives. • Spelling: Check in a dictionary for the correct spelling of words.

FINAL COPY	**Write** • Write the polished final copy of your essay. Read your work one more time before sharing it.

Unit 6: Book Reviews to Book Trailers—Teacher Information

Project Overview

Students will write a book review on a favorite book read during the school year. They will use the review to create a book trailer for the middle-school summer reading program. The book trailer will be shared with students and the community through the classroom web page, blog, or school website.

Project Objectives

When students complete this project, they will be able to
- use the Internet to analyze book trailers.
- write a book review.
- plan and create a book trailer.
- use technology to produce and share book trailers.

Integration of Academic Skills

- Language Arts: write informational text
- Technology: use computer word processing, graphic programs, online resources

Primary Common Core State Standards Addressed

ELA-Literacy.W.6.2 Write informative/explanatory texts to examine a topic and convey ideas, concepts, and information through the selection, organization, and analysis of relevant content.
ELA-Literacy.W.6.6 Use technology, including the Internet, to produce and publish writing as well as to interact and collaborate with others; demonstrate sufficient command of keyboarding skills to type a minimum of three pages in a single sitting.

ELA-Literacy.W.7.2 Write informative/explanatory texts to examine a topic and convey ideas, concepts, and information through the selection, organization, and analysis of relevant content.
ELA-Literacy.W.7.6 Use technology, including the Internet, to produce and publish writing and link to and cite sources as well as to interact and collaborate with others, including linking to and citing sources.

ELA-Literacy.W.8.2 Write informative/explanatory texts to examine a topic and convey ideas, concepts, and information through the selection, organization, and analysis of relevant content.
ELA-Literacy.W.8.6 Use technology, including the Internet, to produce and publish writing and present the relationships between information and ideas efficiently as well as to interact and collaborate with others.

© Copyright 2010. National Governors Association Center for Best Practices and Council of Chief State School Officers. All rights reserved.

Essential Question

How can students promote the middle-school summer reading program?

Type of Project

- ■ Individual Student
- ☐ Collaborative Teams
- ☐ Whole Class

Introductory Event

(This project provides an opportunity for collaboration between the Language Arts teacher and school librarian.)

1. *Scenario:* Research has shown that summer reading programs help teens retain and enhance their reading skills over the summer. Realizing this problem could affect students at our middle school, parents and faculty want to encourage summer reading.
2. *Discussion:* Think about a favorite book you read this year. Do you think others would like to read it? How would you promote it so lots of people would read it?
3. *Discussion:* Have you seen movie trailers that were effective at persuading you to see a movie? What makes them effective? How could you create an effective book trailer that would persuade others to read the book?

Unit 6: Book Reviews to Book Trailers—Teacher Information

Introductory Event (cont.)
4. *Activity:* Students examine online movie and book trailers.
5. *Guest Speaker:* Invite the school librarian to speak about the summer reading program.

Materials/Resources Needed
1. A copy of all handouts for each student: There are several options—paper copy, scan and download handouts to be used on a whiteboard, or post handouts to the classroom web page to be downloaded by students to their laptops.

Technology
1. Computers with word processing, printer, and graphic programs
2. Computers with Internet connections

Internet Tools for Creating a Book Trailer
The following sites offer tools and helpful information for creating book trailers:
URL: <https://www.booktrailersforreaders.com/Home+Student+Trailers>   This site has examples of a variety of student-made book trailers.
URL: <https://getreal.wikispaces.com/technologytools>   This site offers free applications and has detailed instructions on each program listed below.

- Photo Story 3
- iMovie
- PowerPoint
- Mapwings
- Bubble Share
- Voice Thread
- Movie Maker
- Avatars

Managing the Project
Step 1: Launch the Project–Discuss the essential question and complete introductory activities.
Step 2: Review–"Book Review/Book Trailer Project Rubric" handout and "Project Self-Evaluation and Reflection" handout (page 6)
Step 3: Review–"Student Project Planner" handout
Step 4: Activity–Students complete the "Writing a Book Review" handout and use it to write a book review.
Step 5: Activity–View a book trailer and complete "Analyzing Book Trailer Elements" handout.
Step 6: Activity–Students complete "Book Trailer Planner" handout.
Step 7: Activity–Students use the completed "Book Trailer Planner" to complete the "Book Trailer Storyboard" handout.
Step 8: Activity–Students use the completed "Book Trailer Storyboard" handout to create their book trailer. There are several options for creating the book trailer. See the Technology Tools for Creating a Book Trailer section above.
Step 9: Activity–Students share their project with peers and the community. You may want to create a library or classroom web page with links to each team's project.

Project Evaluation
1. The teacher completes the "Book Review/Book Trailer Project Rubric" handout.
2. Students complete the "Project Self-Evaluation and Reflection" handout (page 6).
3. Teacher/student conferences are held to discuss the completed evaluations.

Book Review/Book Trailer Project Rubric

Name: _____ Date: _____

Book Review	Advanced	Proficient	Nearing Proficient	Below Proficient
Content: Fully understands the purpose for writing a book review. Information organized logically. Main characters are mentioned and described; relationships between characters are clear. Plot description is brief, does not give away too much and is clear and easy to follow. After reading the description, the reader is curious about the plot.	4	3	2	1
Organization: Review includes an inviting lead, detailed body, and a conclusion with a recommendation.	4	3	2	1
Mechanics: No grammatical, spelling, or punctuation errors.	4	3	2	1

Book Trailer	Advanced	Proficient	Nearing Proficient	Below Proficient
Book trailer storyboard complete with sketches for each frame, detailed notes about scenes, transitions, and sounds. Trailer hooks the attention of the viewer and keeps it. Plot is revealed just enough to make viewer want to read the book. Images carefully chosen to represent the plot. Soundtrack sets the mood and fully complements text/images. Trailer is between 1–3 minutes long. Copyrighted material cited correctly.	4	3	2	1

Collaboration	Advanced	Proficient	Nearing Proficient	Below Proficient
Uses time effectively in class and focuses on the book trailer project. Always displays positive attitude about the project, never critical of the project or the work of other team members. Consistently works to fulfill project requirements and perform individual team-member role.	4	3	2	1

Teacher Comments:

Unit 6: Book Reviews to Book Trailers— Student Project Planner

Essential Question: How can students promote the middle-school summer reading program?

Project: Write a book review on a favorite book read during the school year. Use the review to create a book trailer. The book trailers for the middle-school summer reading program will be shared with students and the community through the classroom web page, blog, or school website.

Steps

Step 1: Review the "Book Trailer Project Rubric" and "Project Self-Evaluation and Reflection" handouts.

Step 2: Choose a favorite book you have read during the school year and complete the "Writing a Book Review" handout.

Step 3: Write your book review using the completed "Writing a Book Review" handout.

Step 4: Complete the "Analyzing Book Trailer Elements" handout by viewing an online book trailer.

Step 5: Use your book review to complete the "Book Trailer Planner" handout.

Step 6: Use your completed "Book Trailer Planner" handout to complete the "Book Trailer Storyboard" handout.

Step 7: Use your completed "Book Trailer Storyboard" handout to create your book trailer. Choose a computer program such as Photo Story 3 or iMovie. (Consult your teacher for instructions).

Step 8: Share your completed project with students and the community by uploading or linking it to the classroom web page, blog, or school website. (Consult your teacher or librarian for instructions.)

Step 9: Complete the "Project Self-Evaluation and Reflection" handout.

Unit 6: Book Reviews to Book Trailers— Writing a Book Review

A **book review** is a piece of writing to help people decide whether or not the book would interest them enough to read. It is a sneak preview of a book, not a summary. The writer shares his/her opinion about the book, discusses details from the book that support his/her opinion, and makes a recommendation to others. The review follows the format for an essay. A book review has four parts:

- a title that informs
- an introduction with a thesis statement
- the body of the essay
- the conclusion

Directions: Choose a book that you have read during the school year to write an opinion about. Use the guide below to draft your book review. Use a separate sheet of paper to write a draft of your review.

Book Review Guide

1. Write a title for your book review that conveys your overall impression. (ex., "Full of Action and Creepy Characters", "Awesome Illustrations With a Story to Match", etc.).

2. Write a sentence that clearly states, in a strong voice, your opinion of the book.

3. Jot down the pages and passages in the book that you may use to support your opinion.

4. Write a sentence that clearly states, in strong language, your recommendation of the book.

Name: _____ Date: _____

Unit 6: Book Reviews to Book Trailers— Writing a Book Review (cont.)

5. Write a thesis statement. A thesis statement is a complete sentence that tells exactly what you are trying to persuade your readers to believe and why. It is much like a topic sentence in a paragraph.

6. Now expand your thesis statement into a few sentences to make up your beginning paragraph. Begin with an "attention-grabbing" starting sentence. Remember to include the title, author/illustrator, and kind of book it is somewhere within your introductory paragraph.

7. Write the body of the book review. These paragraphs develop the thesis statement and discuss the details from the book that support your opinion (without spoiling the book ending for future readers). Include some of the details about the characters, setting, and theme.

8. Write the conclusion for the book review. Sum up the thesis statement and make recommendations to others in three to four sentences. You may want to give the book a rating. (ex., Five stars: I'm really glad I read it!; One star: I hate it. etc.).

9. When you are satisfied with your book review, make a final copy for publication.

Name: _____ Date: _____

Unit 6: Book Reviews to Book Trailers— Analyzing Book Trailer Elements

Directions: View several online book trailers. Complete the information below by choosing one to analyze.

Setting: Where was the location? Why do you think it was chosen?

Sound Effects/Music: What kind was used?

Words: How were they used? What purpose did they serve?

Visuals: Was it a movie, still images, or a combination?

What do the visuals tell you about what you could expect from reading the book?

Pacing: How was pacing used all through the trailer? About how long was the trailer? Was the time used effectively?

Mood: What kind of mood did the sound, pacing, and words create?

Narrator: Do you know who did the talking? What did you notice about the tone and emotion of the speaker?

Story Highlights: What do you think the book is about? What made you think that?

Rating: With five being the best, how would you rate the effectiveness of the book trailer?

1   2   3   4   5

Explain why you gave it this rating.

Name: _____ Date: _____

Unit 6: Book Reviews to Book Trailers—Book Trailer Planner

Directions: Use your book review and the helpful hints below to plan your book trailer.

Helpful Hints

- Read the blurb on the back of the book. Could you use some of it for your script?
- Think about the main character. Does the character have a favorite saying or motto?
- Build suspense like "A mysterious metallic object hovered over the town."
- Ask a question like "What would you do if....?"

Words: In a few sentences, tell about the story in a way that would make someone want to read it.

_____

_____

_____

_____

_____

_____

_____

_____

Story Highlights: What part of the story will you focus on?

_____

_____

_____

_____

Helpful Hints

- The episode should be near the beginning of the book.
- The episode should show the characters and give a hint of what will happen next.
- The episode should not give away the ending.

Sound Effects/Music: The soundtrack should set the mood and complement your text and images.

_____

_____

_____

Pacing: How will you use pacing? (to draw interest?, show action?, create suspense?). Timing should be effective.

_____

_____

_____

Name: _____ Date: _____

Unit 6: Book Reviews to Book Trailers— Book Trailer Storyboard

A **storyboard** is a visual script of what your book trailer will look like. It shows individual shots (frames) in sequence. Nine frames equals approximately 90 seconds.

Directions: Use your book trailer planner to help you sketch a storyboard for your book trailer. You will need to make several copies of this page to complete your storyboard.

Title of book: _____ Author: _____

Frame # _____

Graphic

Text

_____
_____
_____
_____
_____
_____

Audio

_____
_____

Image Source

_____

Frame # _____

Graphic

Text

_____
_____
_____
_____
_____
_____

Audio

_____
_____

Image Source

_____